W9-AVM-229

CITIZENS' RIGHTS

RIGHTS

A CITIZEN'S GUIDE

Published in the United States of America by Cherry Lake Publishing
Ann Arbor, Michigan
www.cherrylakepublishing.com

Content Adviser: Austin McCoy, Doctoral Candidate in History at the University of Michigan
Reading Adviser: Marla Conn MS, Ed., Literacy specialist, Read-Ability, Inc.

Photo Credits: © Eric Crama/Shutterstock, cover, 1; © Derek Hatfield/Shutterstock, 5; © Joseph Sohm/Shutterstock, 6;
© Africa Studio/Shutterstock, 9; © wavebreakmedia/Shutterstock, 10; © sakhom/Shutterstock, 12; © EdStock/istock, 14;
© tommy japan/Flickr, 17; © Kzenon/Shutterstock, 18; © Photographee.eu/Shutterstock, 20; © Peter Scholz/Shutterstock, 23;
© Sean Pavone/Shutterstock, 24; © Volt Collection/Shutterstock, 27; © 1000 Words/Shutterstock, 28

Library of Congress Cataloging-in-Publication Data
Names: Mara, Wil, author.
Title: Citizens' rights / Wil Mara.
Description: Ann Arbor, Michigan : Cherry Lake Publishing, 2017. | Includes
    bibliographical references and index.
Identifiers: LCCN 2016001517| ISBN 9781634710718 (hardcover) | ISBN 9781634711708
  (pdf) | ISBN 9781634712699 (pbk.) | ISBN 9781634713689 (ebook)
Subjects: LCSH: Civil rights—United States—Juvenile literature.
Classification: LCC JC599.U5 M34 2017 | DDC 323.0973—dc23
LC record available at http://lccn.loc.gov/2016001517

Cherry Lake Publishing would like to acknowledge the work of the Partnership for 21st Century Learning.
Please visit *www.p21.org* for more information.

Printed in the United States of America
Corporate Graphics

ABOUT THE AUTHOR

Wil Mara is an award-winning and best-selling author of more than 150 books, many of which
are educational titles for young readers. Further information about his work can be found at
www.wilmara.com.

TABLE OF CONTENTS

CHAPTER 1

The Foundation of American Citizenship

As citizens of the United States of America, we enjoy rights and privileges that make us unique throughout the world. Millions who came before us fought for this to be possible and act as a reminder that we should never take our way of life for granted. So what are those rights? Who provides them to us? How do they apply to everyday life? Why are they so valuable? And what would it be like to live without them?

To find these answers, one needs to begin with one of the most important documents in America's history: the Constitution. When the Constitution was first drafted in the late 1700s, it outlined the basic principles by which the new nation was to be governed. The first section of the Constitution sets up the rules

The Constitution sets up some basic rules for people who live in the United States.

In a democracy, people vote to elect their leaders.

of government through seven **articles**. This is followed by the Bill of Rights, which is made up of 10 **amendments**. The principles still form the very foundation of American citizenship and the guarantee that our government exists to serve us.

For example, the Constitution divides power into three branches of government: executive, legislative, and judicial. This was done so no single section of government would have too much power, and therefore it would be a government of, by, and for the people. As a result of the ideals laid out in the Constitution, the United States became a powerful example of **democracy**. Many other nations have used it as a model in the centuries since.

21st Century Content

*The right to vote for the leaders of government is perhaps the most important right that America provides. Voting lets your voice be heard, and it is through the vote that ordinary citizens control the way the country runs. Think about it—if you don't like the way your representatives are doing their job, you can vote them out of office! Every elected **politician**—president, senator, governor, mayor, and beyond—has their job because the voters put them there. This is one of the most amazing rights provided by the Constitution.*

CHAPTER 2

The Bill of Rights

There are more than two dozen amendments in the Constitution. But those original 10, the Bill of Rights, form the groundwork for America's **priorities**. This way, citizens have basic protections so that the government doesn't have too much control over their private lives.

Amendment 1

Says that citizens shall have the right to practice their own religion, to exercise freedom of speech, and to assemble (meet in large groups). Examples of this include the right to complain about the government in whatever way they wish—such as through the Internet, magazines, TV, and books. People can

The freedom to practice any religion is protected by the First Amendment.

also gather together in protest against something the government has done or failed to do.

Amendment 2

Says that citizens have the right to bear arms (own guns). This was added in large part in the wake of the oppressive British government, which controlled the colonists in part through military force. The central idea is that an armed citizenry will be able to defend itself should its government rise against it.

As written in the Fifth Amendment, people are "innocent until proven guilty."

Amendment 3

Says that the government can't have soldiers live in people's homes without consent, except in a time of war and then only if **Congress** passes such a law. Again, this was in response to some of the actions taken by the British military, which often demanded that private citizens provide them with food and lodging.

Amendment 4

Says that police and other law enforcement officials must

[21ST CENTURY SKILLS LIBRARY]

obtain legal permission—usually in the form of a **search warrant** from a judge—before entering and searching a person's home. This prevents law enforcement from having the power to randomly invade people's private property without just cause.

Amendment 5

Says that people accused of crimes have some protections. They must be convicted of a crime in court, and they can't be taken to court a second time for the same crime. They don't have to testify against themselves. They also won't lose their property while being tried. In American law, a person is "innocent until proven guilty."

Amendment 6

Says that people accused of a crime have certain rights. They don't have to wait for an unusually long period before having their "day in court." They have a right to know what they are being accused of. Further, the accused people are entitled to obtain witnesses and to know who will act as the witnesses against them.

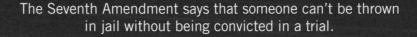

The Seventh Amendment says that someone can't be thrown in jail without being convicted in a trial.

Amendment 7

Says that an accused person is entitled to a trial with a **jury**. It guarantees that anyone convicted of a crime in America has the right to a fair trial. If someone accused is then fined or jailed, the public can be confident that the punishment was the result of a proper trial and not one that was unjust.

Amendment 8

Says that an accused person cannot be made to pay an unnecessarily large fine (such as **bail**) or be subjected to any form of cruel or unusual punishment. This follows the American belief that "the punishment should fit the crime." For example, if you broke a window out of anger, you might have to pay a fine of a few hundred dollars for committing a misdemeanor. That would be a reasonable punishment. Having to go to jail for 10 years, however, would be a bit extreme!

21st Century Content

Capital punishment, also known as the death penalty, is when convicted criminals are put to death. The laws for when this happens are different in each state. Some people who are against capital punishment say that it violates the Eighth Amendment. They say that no matter what crime was committed, executing a criminal counts as "cruel and unusual punishment." Find out what the laws are in your state. What do you think?

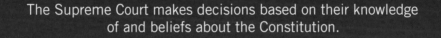

The Supreme Court makes decisions based on their knowledge
of and beliefs about the Constitution.

Amendment 9

Says that American citizens have many rights, and that some
are listed in the Constitution while others are not. You can think
of this as a kind of "junk drawer" amendment. It makes it clear
that Americans may have other rights that aren't listed in the
Constitution. It leaves room for legal interpretation of those other
rights and provides the opportunity for further amendments in
the future.

Amendment 10

Says that the powers not given to the federal government by the Constitution belong to the states and the people. In other words, it limits the power that the government has to what's specified in the Constitution. This is a critically important amendment, because it prevents officials from using more power than they are entitled.

21st Century Content

*The most recent constitutional amendment was fully **ratified** in 1992, after a delay of over 200 years! (It had to do with congressional salaries.) Adding an amendment to the Constitution is not easy. It has to first be proposed by Congress with support from two-thirds of the majority in both the Senate and the House of Representatives, or through a constitutional convention supported by two-thirds of the states. It then has to be ratified by three-fourths of the states—38 of the 50. After a college student realized in 1982 that not enough states had ratified it, he campaigned for more to do it. Maine was the next state to ratify it, followed by 35 more—enough for it to be official.*

CHAPTER 3

Our Rights in Real Life

The Bill of Rights was added to the Constitution on December 15, 1791. The rights granted and the issues they raised are as important today as they were back then. Here are a few examples of those rights being exercised by the American people.

Freedom of Speech

In the late 1960s, during the darkest days of the Vietnam War, three students in Des Moines, Iowa, wore black armbands bearing peace symbols to school. The black symbolized all those who had died during the war, and the peace symbol represented hope that the war would soon be over. The three students were

Here, people protested against President Richard Nixon in the early 1970s.

very young. John Tinker was just 15, his friend Christopher Eckhardt was 16, and John's sister Mary Beth was only 13. They were suspended from school for making such a bold statement against the war, but many felt they had every right to wear the armbands. Their case was called *Tinker v. Des Moines Independent Community School District*, and it went all the way to the U.S. Supreme Court. In 1969, the court decided that the students' First Amendment right to freedom of speech had indeed been violated.

Police need a search warrant before they can enter a house.

Freedom of Religion

Amish people have always believed that their religion permits them to live apart from the influence of the rest of society. For example, they believe education should end after eighth grade. However, many state laws say children must go to school until they are 16 regardless of religion. In a 1972 case called *Wisconsin v. Yoder*, the Supreme Court decided that the First Amendment right to freedom of religion had more power than Wisconsin's law regarding school age. In this way, the Constitution was upheld at the federal level, and the state rule had less power.

[21ST CENTURY SKILLS LIBRARY]

Protection Against Unreasonable Searches and Seizures

In 1957, police in Cleveland, Ohio, received a tip about a criminal suspect hiding at the home of a woman named Dollree Mapp. Eager to catch the suspect, police went to the house and entered without first obtaining a search warrant from a judge. The police didn't find the suspect they wanted, but they did find other materials that were illegal for Mapp to have. She was eventually convicted of being in possession of these materials, but the Supreme Court overturned this conviction. The Supreme Court acknowledged that the materials were illegal for her to have. But they overturned the decision because the police did not have a proper search warrant.

The Right to a Lawyer

A man named Clarence Earl Gideon was charged with burglary in Florida back in 1961. When the case got to court, he asked for a lawyer. However, Florida law did not state that he was entitled to one. Gideon ended up trying to represent himself and was eventually convicted. When the Supreme Court reviewed the case, they ruled that the Sixth Amendment

When someone is arrested, he or she has the right
to remain silent, rather than admit guilt.

had been violated because Gideon had not been able to obtain a new lawyer. Gideon got a new trial with a proper lawyer and was found not guilty.

Life and Career Skills

In 1963, a man named Ernesto Miranda was arrested in Arizona. Police asked him many questions at the time of the arrest. At his trial, the answers Miranda gave formed the only evidence **prosecutors** had to use against him. He was convicted and sentenced to a jail term of up to 30 years. When the Supreme Court reviewed the case later on, it decided to overturn Miranda's conviction because the police failed to inform him that he did not have to answer their questions. This was a violation of Miranda's Fifth Amendment rights. As a result of this case, in 1966, all law enforcement officials became required to give any captured suspect a "Miranda warning." This informs them of their right to remain silent and that anything they say will be used against them in a court of law. Do you feel this is fair, or do you think Miranda's on-the-spot confession should have been considered legal evidence?

CHAPTER 4

Imagine Life Without Those Rights

It's easy to forget that people in other nations don't have the same freedoms that Americans do. Too often in the past (and even today in some places), people around the world have been denied these rights. One of the most notable recent examples was in the old Soviet Union, most of which is now occupied by the country of Russia.

Throughout much of the 20th century, people in the former Soviet Union had to be very careful about everything they said. Speaking out against the government was extremely dangerous, and the government had many spies walking among the population in search of "traitors." Soviet citizens knew to be careful because, as the saying went, "the walls have ears." The Soviet government owned all the newspapers as well as the radio

Mikhail Gorbachev was the last leader of the Soviet Union before it collapsed.

and TV stations. Reporters, therefore, only wrote and said the most positive things about the government. Punishments for doing otherwise could be harsh, including steep fines, beatings, jail time, and even death.

In the late 1980s and early 1990s, the people of the Soviet Union rose up against their government. Even though they didn't have a Bill of Rights to protect them, they decided they'd had enough and were going to make changes. They held huge protests in the streets—exercising exactly the kind of "right to assemble" that is guaranteed in the U.S. Constitution. Even when soldiers

Tiananmen Square was the site of a huge protest in 1989.

and tanks appeared to scare these people off, the frustrated
citizens stood their ground. By late 1991, the Soviet Union
collapsed and was eventually split into more than a dozen smaller
countries.

The people of the Soviet Union were eventually able to make
changes in their country and start down the road to having the
same personal freedoms Americans enjoy every day. Citizens of
other countries, sadly, have not been so lucky.

On April 15, 1989, college students in Beijing, China, held a public gathering to honor the memory of a dead government leader who had supported democracy. This gathering inspired more pro-democracy supporters. A few weeks later, about 100,000 students, workers, and others held a march in support of democracy and freedom of the press. Soon there were mass gatherings in about 400 cities across the country. The Chinese government became worried that they were losing control of their citizens. On the night of June 3, the Chinese military stormed into Tiananmen Square, where thousands of people had gathered. As many as 5,000 were eventually killed in the massacre that followed. To this day, it remains one of the most disturbing examples of oppressive governance in human history—and evidence as to why personal rights are so important.

CHAPTER 5

Safeguarding Our Rights

Think of how many privileges come with being an American. The right to say whatever you like about your government. The right to go to whatever church, mosque, synagogue, or other house of worship you wish. The right to be properly represented and tried in court if you are accused of a crime. And there are so many other rights, including those found in state and local laws. Continue to study those rights, and you will better understand your place in the world and become a smart, responsible citizen.

Also remember that the rights provided by the Constitution aren't simply there to outline the rules of American citizenship—they're also there to protect you. In other words, they don't simply

The more you know, the more power you have.

If you feel strongly about an issue, speak up!

tell you what you can and can't do, they tell you what others can and can't do to you. And if you ever feel as though your constitutional rights have been violated, you have many options to seek justice.

And remember—the 26th Amendment to the Constitution lowered the voting age to 18. Prior to that, you had to be 21 to cast your vote in an election, but now you can have a voice in the choosing of your political leaders while still a teenager! So you better start learning about the issues that concern you, as well as where the **candidates** stand on them. Because at that point, you won't just be learning about democracy anymore— you'll be part of it!

21st Century Content

Rock the Vote is an organization that started in 1990. It partners with MTV and encourages people to register to vote as soon as they turn 18. Many celebrities have filmed videos in support of it, including Justin Timberlake, Kendall Jenner, will.i.am, and Miley Cyrus.

Think About It

Read about a recent criminal case in the news. Then reread Chapter 2. Which amendments relate to what happened? Were anyone's rights violated?

Writing is one way that people exercise their freedom of speech. Authors share their beliefs and ask their readers to think in new ways. But in some places, like North Korea, the government controls which books can be published. Can you imagine some ways this affects the people who live there?

For More Information

BOOKS

Krull, Kathleen, and Anna DiVito (illustrator). *A Kid's Guide to America's Bill of Rights*. New York: HarperCollins, 2015.

Steinkraus, Kyla. *The Constitution*. Vero Beach, FL: Rourke, 2015.

Winter, Jonah, and Barry Blitt (illustrator). *The Founding Fathers! The Horse-Ridin', Fiddle-Playin', Book-Readin', Gun-Totin' Gentlemen Who Started America*. New York: Atheneum, 2015.

ON THE WEB

Congress for Kids—The Three Branches of Government
http://www.congressforkids.net/Constitution_threebranches.htm

Kids.gov—Government
https://kids.usa.gov/government/index.shtml

PBS Kids—The Democracy Project: President for a Day
http://pbskids.org/democracy/be-president/

GLOSSARY

amendments (uh-MEND-muhnts) changes made to a bill

articles (AHR-ti-kuhls) pieces of a legal document that each deal with a single topic

bail (BAYL) money paid to a court for the release of someone accused of a crime, with the promise that he or she will show up for the trial

candidates (KAN-di-dates) people who are running for office in an election

Congress (KAHNG-gris) the lawmaking body of the United States, made up of the Senate and the House of Representatives

democracy (dih-MAH-kruh-see) a form of government in which the people choose their leaders in elections

jury (JOOR-ee) a group of people, usually 12 in number, who listen to the facts at a trial and decide whether the accused person is innocent or guilty

politician (pah-lih-TISH-uhn) a person who runs for or holds a government office

priorities (prye-OR-ih-teez) things that are more important or more urgent than other things

prosecutors (PRAH-sih-kyoo-turz) lawyers who represent the government in criminal trials

ratified (RAT-uh-fyed) approved officially

search warrant (SURCH WOR-uhnt) an order from a court that allows the police to enter and search a place

INDEX